The Road Less Traveled

Larry Mast

THE ROAD LESS TRAVELED

Copyright © 2023 Larry Mast

Published by Book Ripple Publishing
www.BookRipple.com

All rights reserved. No part of this book may be reproduced or transmitted in any form or by any means, electronic or mechanical, including photocopying and recording, or by an information storage and retrieval system, without permission in writing from the publisher.

All Scripture quotations, unless otherwise indicated, are taken from the Holy Bible, New International Version®, NIV®. Copyright ©1973, 1978, 1984, 2011 by Biblica, Inc.™ Used by permission of Zondervan. All rights reserved worldwide. www.zondervan.com The "NIV" and "New International Version" are trademarks registered in the United States Patent and Trademark Office by Biblica, Inc.™

Cover photo by Brian Mast. All other photos by Larry or Helen Mast, unless otherwise noted.
Cover design by Abraham Mast.

ISBN: 978-1-951797-96-6
Printed in the United States of America

To reach the author, go to:
www.LarryMast.com

"... Two roads diverged in a wood,
and I, I took the one less traveled by,
And that has made all the difference."
– Robert Frost

INTRODUCTION

I wrote the letter below for my friend, Mark Ottey, in Montana, and included this book-cover photo of Mt. Elbert in Colorado. Mark was near the end of his life after a four-year battle with cancer. I lived in Texas and was deeply concerned about his eternal future.

*** *** ***

Hello Mark, April 30, 2021

The photo is of me on Mt. Elbert in September 2005. This 14,433-foot mountain is the highest in Colorado.

During late summer 2005, I was recovering from cerebral malaria, which I had picked up in Sierra Leone, West Africa, earlier in the year. In the August heat I told Helen, "I need to get out of Texas!" Naturally, I thought of the mountains. I drove to Colorado Springs and stayed with friends. Our son Brian lived in Florida at the time and made a business trip to Dallas. He then flew to Colorado and joined me. I wish our son Brad could have come, too, but he couldn't get away.

On our first afternoon on the mountain, Brian and I climbed to the tree line and set up camp. That evening we made a campfire, ate food, told stories, ate more food, and went to bed at dark. I was glad for a warm sleeping bag at 12,000 feet.

In the morning we stashed our tent and sleeping bags in the brush and set out at six a.m. for the summit. Mt. Elbert is not a technical climb, just a long hike at high altitude. I was not totally well yet, so I was glad to let my 35-year-old son carry my backpack occasionally. Other people passed us since we weren't setting any land-speed records.

So many hikers have used the upper reaches of the trail that it looks almost like a road. We reached the summit about ten a.m. More than a dozen hikers stood around the peak, most on their cell phones!

Brian took this photo as we started our descent. I had quoted Robert Frost's poem *The Road Not Taken,* on our ascent, so when Brian sent me the photo later in a frame, I was pleased to see he'd incorporated Frost's poetry as a fitting tribute to our efforts.

In some ways the poem exemplifies my life as well. I've certainly been in some

Mark Ottey
Photo credit: April Ottey

rough terrain in out-of-the-way places! But there never was a time when I walked alone. I always sensed the Lord was there to help carry the load.

Mark, my mountain climbing companion and friend of almost fifty years, you are nearing the end of your trail on this earth. But I'm not sure of one thing—is Jesus Christ your best friend, companion, and Savior as you enter eternity? I know we've talked about this before. Please let me explain one more time. It's not as hard as you think.

Do you remember our recent conversation about Lazarus? Jesus, the man who loved Lazarus, Mary, and Martha, and wept when Lazarus died, loves you, too. We are all sinners, and our good life and deeds are not enough to get us into heaven. We must simply accept Christ's death on the cross as payment for our sins and thank Him for the gift of new life in Christ. God, who made the mountains, rivers, and valleys, made a way for man, also His creation, to enter His presence forever.

Join me, my friend! There is room on the trail beside me. Join me on the road less traveled—that leads to heaven. Hope to see you there!

Your friend, Larry

*** *** ***

Mark did choose to follow Jesus shortly before his death on June 17, 2021. His wife Connie graciously gave me permission to publish my letter to him.

Acknowledgments

An enormous thank you to our son Brian who provided the cover photo from Colorado, along with his usual expertise as editor, publisher, and advisor.

Thanks to our son Brad for our photo on the back cover.

A heartfelt thank you to the Writing Group led by Sandi Tompkins. Your encouragements, edits, and suggestions were very helpful. The team varied so much over the years, I won't mention any names. You know who you are.

Many thanks to the prayer team that kept us uplifted in prayer.

Thanks to my wonderful wife Helen. This book would not be a reality without you. Thank you for all your work. You typed, edited, and retyped, as we created this together. I love you.

Most of all we thank God who leads us daily.

Contents

#1 Done & Faithful Servant	12
#2 Remember the Incredible Hulk?	14
#3 Brother Hussein's Smile	16
#4 The Call from Barn Janey	18
#5 My Friend the Wren	21
#6 One Elusive Evening	23
#7 What Time Is It, Ernie?	28
#8 Bowling with Ernie	30
#9 Vulnerable	35
#10 Asleep in the Back of a U-Haul	39
#11 Duck While You Can	43
#12 The Hill	45
#13 Why Am I Here?	49
#14 Edgar Goes Home	52
#15 And Then … Paula Smiled	54
#16 The Rock	61
#17 Canadian Rescue	64
#18 Mmmmm … Mayonnaise	68
#19 Sparkling Clean & Streak Free	70
#20 United Airlines Flight 950	73
#21 Possum Dance	75
#22 More Important than a Box	77

#23 WHEN MERCY COMES FULL CIRCLE	80
#24 REMEMBERING REYNITA	85
#25 REDEEMING THE WALL	87
#26 CHRISTMAS CAROLING	89
#27 A GIFT FOR EDNA	95
#28 A GOOD WEEK FOR HUNTING	99
#29 ANY POST IN A STORM	103
#30 FOLLOW DIRECTIONS	106
#31 FOLLOW ME	108
#32 GLUE MAKERS STICKING IT TO US	110
#33 HAPPY LANDING	113
#34 I JUST RAN OVER A LITTLE BOY	115
#35 IT'S HERE!	120
#36 KNICKERBOCKER REPORT	124
#37 LIFE LESSONS FROM A SKUNK	127
#38 MEANGUERA ISLAND, EL SALVADOR	130
#39 MR. TRACE	133
#40 PEPSI GENERATION	135
#41 PECANS & PERSEVERANCE	139
#42 TELLTALE TAIL TRAIL	141
#43 THE BLAME GAME	144
#44 THE DOCTOR IS IN	146
#45 THE MAN IN THE RED CAR	149
#46 THE STORY OF THE ANCHOR	151
#47 WHEN WORDS FAIL YOU	156

DONE & FAITHFUL SERVANT

In 1992 my wife Helen and I were serving onboard the Mercy Ship *Anastasis,* in Sierra Leone, West Africa. It was a lengthy commitment in the country, made longer when the ship boiler broke down. The boiler was necessary to heat the heavy fuel for sailing, so we waited in port and continued our field service until a boiler replacement arrived from Scotland. Air conditioning had not yet been installed on the ship, so cabins were hot and sleep at night very difficult.

The crew felt it on all levels. One evening during the weekly community meeting on aft deck, CEO Simonne Dyer spoke from Matt. 25:21 with the familiar words, "Well done, good and faithful servant." When she quoted the verse, however, she inadvertently switched several words around and said, "Well good, done and faithful servant ... enter into the joy of the Lord."

I looked around. From my place in the back, I could see that most people hadn't even noticed it. Simonne's son Mark, though, sitting nearby, was cracking up. Yes, we were all very tired, "done in," with the heat, stress and labor of the extended field service.

As I've thought about it more, maybe it was appropriate, a divine moment of communication. "Well done" paints a picture of an assigned task completed with excellence. I'm glad the Lord used those two simple and powerful words. His "well done" commendation was not to the well established, the well-to-do, the well connected, or the well known. He doesn't care if you're well dressed, well fed, well traveled or even well intentioned.

The Lord only asks that you be faithful to the work He gave you in life. And, if you arrive at your destination well used and well worn, that's okay, too. Then the Lord might say, "Well good, done and faithful servant, enter into the joy of the Lord."

#2
REMEMBER THE INCREDIBLE HULK?

In 2010, I was part of a team from Mercy Ships involved with hurricane relief work in the Texas gulf area. One of our volunteer teams was a group of Church of Christ students from the University of Tennessee. Helen and I later visited them at their campus ministry night in Knoxville, where the speaker shared this story.

*** *** ***

"When my younger brother David was ten-years old, he liked to watch *The Incredible Hulk* on television. He loved it, lived it, and even dreamed it.

"One evening our family went shopping, that is, all of us except David. Mother tried to get him to go, but he wanted to stay home. Since we wouldn't be gone long, mother finally relented.

"When we returned, we couldn't find David anywhere. He wasn't in the living room, kitchen, or his bedroom. We finally saw a gleam of light under the bathroom door. Mom opened the door and there stood David, as green as he could possibly get. He had used mother's makeup, mascara, and anything else he could find that would make him a shade of green. He had cut up his good t-shirt as well, and now stood admiring himself in the mirror.

"Mother was upset to say the least, about her expensive makeup and the shredded t-shirt. She bawled him out good, but David replied with a deadpan Incredible Hulk voice: 'Mom, don't make me angry. You wouldn't like me when I'm angry.'

"Now mother was thoroughly exasperated. She got out the paddle and took David into her bedroom. I eavesdropped at the door because I wanted to hear him get a good spanking, since he was a pain in the neck most of the time. However, as the paddling began, all I heard from David was 'Gr-r-r-r-r. Gr-r-r-r-r.'"

#3

BROTHER HUSSEIN'S SMILE

This story was written in the 1970's while we served in a strict Muslim nation. Helen and I, plus our two young sons, were part of a Medical Mission in Yemen. I was the "muhendis" ... Arabic for engineer, and was expected to fix anything and everything.

*** *** ***

Answering a request from one of our nurses, I gathered my tools and went to repair a gate in the crowded clinic waiting area. I made my way through the people who sat on the ground. I took care to keep the hanging tools on my nail apron from hitting their heads. It was wall-to-wall people with much chattering, shouting, and crying babies. The swinging gate that needed repair didn't take long. I added a brace to stiffen it and tightened the spring to close it.

I looked down at my feet as I walked back through the crowd to avoid stepping on fingers or toes. Then I nearly bumped into a man who stood in my way. My eyes rose to his face and to the gentle smile that is so characteristic of Hussein, a secret believer. Our eyes met, we shook hands and greeted each other as I paused briefly on my way through the watching crowd.

While I looked into his eyes, it was as if we shared a secret as deep as eternity. In those dark brown eyes I plainly saw love, discretion, and a tender heart ready to do the Master's will. In that moment our spirits touched and I felt a thrill in my soul as I anticipated the day we would meet again in Heaven. Perhaps we will sit and visit by the river. There will be no danger or language barrier. But then, we had no language barrier today, either.

#4

THE CALL FROM BARN JANEY

In 1992, Mercy Ships opened a National Office in Lausanne, Switzerland, and needed a carpenter to do some remodeling. My wife and I spent eight months there while I worked on the beautiful old chalet.

*** *** ***

One day we met Janey Porchet. She and her husband Roger had a small farm just outside Lausanne. They allowed Mercy Ships to store used furniture in an old barn on their property. We made numerous trips to the barn to deliver or pick up furniture and always enjoyed Janey's friendship and hospitality. Since Helen and I had another acquaintance named Jane, we affectionately called this Jane "Barn Janey."

In January 2012, we sent the Porchets a copy of my first book, *Staying on the Trail Through Trials.* A few weeks later Janey phoned from her home in Switzerland. She and Roger had recently suffered some misfortunes. Roger spent three weeks in the hospital following pancreatic cancer surgery. Immediately after he returned home, he fell and broke his hip.

Janey had two strokes and said her short-term memory was going fast. In addition, her eyesight had grown worse and she knew she would eventually go blind. This is especially hard because she loves to read, sketch, and drive her car.

Janey said they had few friends left in the area and it meant so much to receive the book. She sat up several nights and read, laughed, and cried. The font was big enough for her to read. We had prayed over the smallest details of the book, including font size.

Janey ended with these words, "You will never know how much your book helped. It was like it was written just for me."

Helen asked if she could pray with her over the phone. As she prayed clearly and slowly so Janey could understand, I thought, *this is what it's all about. I don't write for fame and fortune, but to help, encourage, and bless people.*

As we once stored furniture in a Swiss barn, so I will forever store Janey's phone call in my Swiss memory bank.

My Friend the Wren

Someone jokingly asked me if I thought a cat could "dog" a man's footsteps? Yes, I believe so—I've seen a cat following closely behind his master, tail erect as a flagpole, at full attention. Of course, we don't really know what any cat is thinking. He could have been surreptitiously planning an attack on the man's leg.

But can a bird "dog" a man's footsteps? The answer is yes. Last winter I had a Carolina Wren follow me around while I split firewood. He found some of the blocks had bugs, termites, and larvae in them. Soon he showed up whenever he heard my sledgehammer ring on the steel wedge. It must have sounded like a dinner bell. He landed on each newly split block of wood, often coming within three or four feet of me. He probably associated me with food, and thinks I'm the greatest thing that happened since God created worms.

Today I was building a cedar wall out in the yard. The wren, whom I named Wilberforce, came to check things out. He hopped under the lumber stacked across my wheelbarrow, and I could hear him pecking inside. He sits about four feet away now and isn't even bothered when I use the noisy power saw.

I'm talking to him nowadays, like: "Wilberforce, what are you doing here? You could get hurt, you know."

That might be a bad sign—talking to a bird. But he just cocked his head to one side and said, "My name isn't Wilberforce, I'm Richard the Lionheart."

ONE ELUSIVE EVENING

#6

Buck Hawkins is his name. I met him one March evening while on a trip to Florida. Even his name suggests "cowboy," and Buck is all of that, from hat to boot heels, though at 92, he doesn't ride horses anymore. When Buck turned 89 he gave up his daily rides and put his horse out to pasture. He's in the Florida Cowboy Hall of Fame, but I'll always remember him for a couple hours spent in the back of his jeep, rambling across his 3,000-acre ranch.

Sometimes those magic moments slip up on you unexpectedly, and at other times, you can make them happen. A friend of mine had suggested we "throw Buck in his jeep and look over his ranch some evening." Buck uses a walker now and doesn't "throw" well, but we managed to hoist him in, get him buckled up, and while my friend drove, we entered a corner of paradise.

I was the gate opener, and there were 14 of them as we crisscrossed the ranch. At the first gate, and off to one side, stood a short plywood wall, oddly discordant in the lush landscape. "The game warden hides behind that," Buck explained, "waiting for poachers." I could see why. White-tailed deer scattered several directions and an alligator floated nearby, half submerged in a water-filled ditch. A mixed breed of beef cattle spread out ahead of us. With the groves of trees, palmettos and frequent ponds, I still had a sense of grassy expanse, green from an abundant rainfall.

Wild Irises showed off their lavender beauty, while Water Hyacinths waited their turn. Wild pigs foraging for food had plowed bone-jarring craters in the meadows. Ahead of us, a sow called her litter as we approached, and little multicolored piglets ran to the safety of their mother's side. Buck never complained about the ride, even when we circled a reedy lake to look for ducks and got into multiple craters made by wild pigs.

A lone cow stood near the fence, her newborn calf at her feet. His first attempt to stand ended in a nosedive.

The scent of orange blossoms overlay the ranch, drifting in from some distant orchard. I had a sensation of unreality and a bittersweet knowledge that I would not "pass this way again," at least never quite like this. Not even a mosquito spoiled this Eden! My thoughts were interrupted by a splash, as a large gator launched himself from an embankment, sending waves the length of the pond. "Must have been a ten-footer!" Buck quipped. Gators occasionally catch and eat the young calves.

A stately pair of Sandhill Cranes moved out of our way, followed by two small yellow balls of fluff. Their parents must have looked like skyscrapers to them! Egrets followed the cows, looking for grasshoppers stirred by the cow's feet, and Great Blue Herons and White Herons fished the shallows. A Meadowlark sang from a fencepost and a Red-winged Blackbird took up the tenor.

Buck seemed pleased to get away from the confines of his home and the limitations of his walker. Though a poor second to his horse, his jeep put him in touch again with his beloved ranch. He knew it all like the back of his work-hardened hand, and he took delight in sharing it with us. The fences, ponds, ditches and canals; he had

Buck Hawkins
Photo credit: Bradley Mast

put them in since he bought the land for five dollars an acre over 50 years ago. Every year on his birthday, Buck puts on a barbecue party at his ranch, attended by over 400 guests. Next February I am invited.

The padlock on the last gate snapped shut in the fading sunset and we headed north on Route 72. Hunched in the back of the jeep, gripping the roll bar, mud from the tires hit me in the face. Car lights began to come on and I knew the idyllic evening was over. One hundred miles to the northeast, the lights of Disney's Magic Kingdom were no doubt coming on over a noisy and jostling crowd. However, in the wind-whipped darkness, I was content, for I had met a man at home and at peace with his land.

#7

WHAT TIME IS IT, ERNIE?

In April 1970, my father-in-law, Ernie Swartz, and I traveled up the Alaska Highway. We drove an old blue GMC van, and pulled a small sleeper trailer. Ernie and I traded places behind the wheel, day and night, straight through from Pennsylvania into Canada, and got on the Alaska-Canada (Alcan) Highway in Dawson Creek, British Columbia.

Halfway up the Alcan, we decided to get a good night's rest. A wooded turn out looked inviting so we pulled off the road and parked our rig. We ate supper prepared on a small propane stove and headed for bed. I would sleep in the trailer and Ernie in the back of the van. He agreed to wake me about six a.m. so we could get an early start.

It seemed just a short time before he banged on the door. It was still very dark. Ernie said he'd make breakfast while I got dressed. In the process of pulling on my shoes, I forced my eyes open enough to look at my watch—it said twelve o'clock!

At breakfast I asked why we got up at midnight instead of six a.m. The problem was discovered when Ernie looked carefully at his watch—it was on upside down! We decided to go anyway, since we were already up and finished breakfast. Actually, I made *him* drive—I crawled back on his bed and went to sleep!

Ernie, with his first great-grandson, Abraham.

#8

BOWLING WITH ERNIE

On a winter's jaunt to Sarasota, Florida, Helen and I visited her parents, Ernie and Naomi Swartz. One afternoon I felt "coerced" into bowling with my father-in-law, a very competitive 83-year-old, and his group of seniors.

*** *** ***

I hadn't bowled in about 30 years, but I hoped those skills would quickly return. At the bowling alley that afternoon I strode to the line and, on my very first try, rolled a perfect gutter-ball! Right in front of Dad Swartz and Bill and Mary and John and Pal and Rosie and Jo. I felt about six inches high as I rolled the ball a second time, then crawled confidently back to my chair.

I think I hit three pins on my second try, but at least it wasn't another gutter ball. My score for the first game was an amazing 76! Since it was obvious I wasn't going to set any records, I turned to one of my favorite pastimes—people watching.

For this diversion I naturally picked on my bowling companions. First of all, I chose Big John. His pre-throw stance caught my attention. Holding the ball high, he took deadly aim, then his ankles began to move from side to side and up and down. This movement then rose above his socks until his legs quivered and vibrated. Finally, he began his forward motion. But—no! After one step he stopped, as if he had forgotten something, maybe milk or bread at the grocery store, then he finished his delivery. This happened EVERY time. Watching Big John helped me forget my score.

Mary more or less walked to the line and dropped the ball. Fortunately, she always missed her foot, and believe it or not, the ball rolled to the other end! While I threw the bowling ball at fourteen or fifteen mph, hers meandered down the alley at five or six. Nevertheless, during the afternoon she made more than one strike.

"Lavender Bill" was suave and cool looking, wore lavender shorts and a color-coordinated shirt, and resembled a riverboat gambler. He was a good bowler and even offered me some advice—how to stand, which arrow on the floor to aim at, etc. Unfortunately, it didn't help much. I stood on the third red dot from the right side and aimed at the third arrow in the distance, but the ball still had a close affinity for the gutter! I suggested to Dad Swartz that we use one of those bowling lanes for beginners with little railings on the sides, but he just laughed at me.

I believe I figured out the secret of the whole thing, anyway. To do well at bowling you must wear white socks. Everybody in Ernie's team had on white socks except Pal, and he had on a white shirt, which helped him somehow. I had on the wrong color socks, so there was no way I could compete.

Ernie bowled 146—low for him, I think, because he was trying to instruct his son-in-law on the finer points of bowling. He didn't want me to bring shame on the family name. I'm proud to say I bowled 104 on the second game and only regressed to 101 on game three. Perhaps bowling is too strenuous for me at my tender age of fifty-seven years.

Just so you can get to know Ernie a little better, let me end with this story. I was trying to fix a stubborn plumbing problem in the Swartz' bathroom. The project required several trips downtown for parts. At one hardware store, Ernie and I searched in vain for what we needed.

When we were ready to leave the store, we found ourselves trying to get out a glass door that wouldn't open, one that said "Entrance Only" on the other side. You know—the aggravating type of door with no handle where you need one. A four-foot railing extended some twelve feet back into the store between the entrance and exit sides. The woman at the cash register saw our predicament and said, "You'll have to come back around and use the exit door."

So, like a good citizen, I retraced my steps. NOT ERNIE! He grasped the railing with both hands and in one smooth fluid motion, he vaulted over and was out the door long before me. The clerk just smiled. I hope I'm vaulting railings when I'm 83 years old. In fact, I hope my bowling score improves with age.

Photo credit: Jim Bayles

VULNERABLE

No one had pets at our remote mission station in Yemen. A few stray dogs from Muharraq Village hung around our houses looking for table scraps. But they were thin, sickly, and often covered with scabs and sores. Some had rabies. A cat for our six and eight-year-old boys to play with would be welcome.

*** *** ***

I felt its eyes upon me before I saw the cat. Then a furtive grey movement in the far corner of my woodshop suddenly disappeared.

The next day the feral cat was back, sitting fearfully in a far corner. Its eyes were intense and blazing. My sudden movement sent it leaping out the open window. Could it ever be tamed?

Early the next morning I set out a small bowl with a couple tablespoons of powdered milk mixed in water. I watched the cat appear like a grey shadow and lap up the milk. Then she was gone.

Over the next couple months of milk and patience the cat calmed down considerably. She tolerated my presence and the noise of table saw and hammer. The day came when she let me stroke her back briefly, before she turned tail and ran. But a level of trust had been achieved. The cat accepted me—but not our active and noisy boys. Not yet.

One day I fed my furry friend her morning milk and knelt down on the dirt floor to pet her. She arched her back and purred her appreciation. Then she laid down and rolled over.

I will never forget what happened next. Thinking she wanted me to rub her stomach, I stroked her with my right hand. Suddenly she must have realized she was in an extremely vulnerable position, for she sank her teeth deep into the palm of my hand! Then she jumped up and vanished around the corner. I had four bleeding puncture wounds in my right hand. One of the nurses cleaned the wound and wrapped my hand.

The cat returned after a few days and the taming process began again. I never reached my final goal, however, because our family left Yemen for Arabic language study in Amman, Jordan.

The end of the story was related to me later by Mike Babbage, the Australian doctor at our mission station. The cat turned into a pet and lived on our compound. Mike told me that one evening at dusk he went to step out of his house in his customary sandals. Before his foot hit the ground, the cat attacked and killed a very poisonous snake coiled right where he would have stepped. Mike thought the cat may have saved his life.

*** *** ***

Are you vulnerable today, in a good way? Do you let people get close to you or are you remote, professional, and emotionally distant? I grew up in a western Montana culture where "Real men don't cry." But Jesus wept, and if He did, so can I. The Bible says, "Weep with those who weep." One of my consistent prayers is *Lord, break my heart for what breaks yours.* You can't go wrong with that.

The next time you're "on your back" with sorrow or pain and someone reaches out to help you, don't "bite them" and run away. Don't reject their care and love, but let them comfort you. A few soft strokes of God's love won't hurt you at all.

Vulnerability softens our hearts. Compassion grows in a softened heart, and compassion can save the lives of many around you about to be bitten by that snake Satan.

#10
ASLEEP IN THE BACK OF A U-HAUL

Sarasota, Florida, beckons. How soon we forget the snow and cold of the north, as our tires hum down I-75. Tonight, my wife Helen and I will relax with family in Pinecraft, a suburb of Sarasota. Tomorrow we dine at Der Dutchman, an Amish restaurant known far and wide for fine food, not to mention 17 varieties of homemade pie!

In my fast lane reverie, I prepare to pass a U-Haul truck, driving slightly slower in the right-hand lane. What I see stops me in my tracks, or I should say stops my daydreams of key lime or peanut butter pies. *The large back door of the U-Haul is wide open, and a young lady lies sound asleep very near the edge of the truck bed. If she turns over in her sleep, she will very likely fall to her death.*

I slow and pull in behind. What should we do? Call 911? Or pull alongside and signal the driver? Honk the horn to wake her up? No, that may cause the very thing we don't want to happen. We follow along for a while, praying for her and the driver. Is her husband driving, and is she so tired she needs to get out of the cab and stretch out for a nap?

Finally, we take a photo, ease around the truck, and continue down I-75 to family, fun, and pecan pie. Because we didn't know what to do, we did nothing.

Now, twenty-five years later, I think that is what bothers me: we didn't know what to do and did nothing. There must have been a "best option." That long ago, we

didn't have cell phones, so we couldn't call 911. Perhaps, someday, someone will read this story, see the photo, and send us a text saying, "I was that lady in the back of the U-Haul truck. Thanks for your prayers!"

The Lord gave me a quite different word picture to draw a closure and restore a sense of peace. How often do we walk near the edge of a "precipice" in life and not even know we are in danger? It's not that we are asleep, we just don't see the whole picture. Would that I could rest so comfortably in the Lord's care that I am never anxious or worried though danger and fear is all around me.

I end with a poem called *Edges*, by Seth Marlin.

> When I walk to the edge
> Of all the light I have
> And take that step into
> The darkness of the unknown
> I believe one of two things will happen;

There will be something
Solid for me to stand on
Or I will be taught to fly!

#11
Duck While You Can

When I was in Grade School our favorite recess activity was playing softball. My position was catcher. I liked the constant action and could throw hard to the bases.

*** *** ***

One morning recess we were in the middle of an exciting softball game. My cousin, Gerald Kauffman, was pitching and I was catcher. We had a runner at first who looked like he wanted to steal second. Mrs. Dyer, strictest English teacher I ever had, was the umpire, and she liked to stand behind the pitcher. Gerald pitched, and I don't remember if it was a ball or strike, for that is all lost in what immediately followed. The runner headed for second and I fired the ball as hard as I could to the second baseman. Gerald ducked. Mrs. Dyer didn't.

I still remember the hollow "thunk" as it hit her high on the chest and bounced away. I was speechless. Nobody laughed; all went deathly quiet. Mrs. Dyer was crimson with anger (or maybe pain) as she immediately ended the recess and ordered us back into the classroom. No speech followed and nobody was even reprimanded, but we were a subdued bunch of students as we went back to diagramming sentences. Oh, maybe we smirked a little bit, but not in *her* sight!

Years later I visited Mrs. Dyer in a retirement home in Montana. She was in her 90's then, and we talked about a lot of things that happened in grade school. But not *that* ballgame. Some things are better left unsaid.

#12

THE HILL

By special invitation we came, five spectators to Lehman Auditorium. The room stood empty, but for eight people who practiced under the stage lights. We five family members filed in and sat together in the center, halfway back.

We would view the practice tonight for next weekend's 100-year home-coming celebration of Eastern Mennonite University (EMU) in Harrisonburg, Virginia. Helen's brother, one of the players on stage, arranged for us to watch the evening presentation. The actors planned to revisit much of the history of the university in a light-hearted but intense and stimulating manner. No small endeavor.

EMU holds special meaning for me. There, in the fall of 1963, as a 20-year-old freshman, I met my future wife. Even more significantly, it was there, one autumn night on the hill behind the college that I rededicated my life to Jesus. I can take you to the spot, I can take you to the place—little has changed except for a gravel pathway criss-crossing the hill and a couple landscape additions.

I could tell you of my friend Dick Heatwole who prayed with me. I could tell you of the intense spiritual battle fought on the side of that grassy hill. I could ... but wait, I need to pay attention to the homecoming storyline acted out on the stage in front of me.

A pretend TV Game Show took place, complete with bells and whistles, as contestants on stage responded to the show host. The guy on the left stool always rang his bell first, though he seldom had the right answer. All part of the game—to entertain the crowd.

Then the venue changed to favorite places on campus. My thoughts drifted ... I heard Maplewood Dorm, Oakwood Dorm, the library, the cafeteria, but to my surprise, the all-time favorite place was *the hill*. It can't be ... that's *my* hill! Though it seems it was a special place for many people.

The stories went on, and I grew restless. Over the years I returned many times to the hill behind the college, to reminisce and renew my vows to God. I had never returned at night. I planned to go in the morning. *Why not now?*

I excused myself from our group and left the auditorium. Outside it was dark with a fall chill in the air. I made my way up the hill to the same spot where, 54 years earlier, I surrendered my life to God and the mission field. The night stars were my witness, the glimmer and glow of Harrisonburg my stage lights. It was here, long ago, after hours of struggle that I begged Dick to sing something. In his rich baritone voice he sang *Just As I Am.* The tears fell as my heart's door opened wide.

Tonight I sang a verse of *Just As I Am* into the darkness and once again rededicated my life to God. I was alone, except for a couple flashlights, like fireflies, on the hilltop. They eventually crossed the hill to a student gathering at the Planetarium.

I made my way back down to Lehman Auditorium and the play in progress. As I opened the door I could almost hear the Heavenly Stage Master say, "Well done, good and faithful servant" ... but then the muted sound of voices on the stage brought me back down to earth where I belong ... *till the play is over.*

› #13

WHY AM I HERE?

Why am I here?
I asked myself that question in El Salvador
At the Mercy Ship's Clinic on a 100-degree afternoon.
And then I noted what I was not ...
I was not a doctor, nurse, or physician's assistant,
Nor a translator, guitar player or clown.
I don't do balloons or puppets,
I'm not the life of the party.
Lord, why am I here?

That afternoon at the clinic I saw a little girl
Sitting on someone's knee
And wished she had come to me.
I turned and went inside to write stories for donors,
Reports for newsletters, etcetera ...
At least I could do that.
And then I prayed,

*Lord, would You do something special
today
Just for me?*

In just a few minutes that same little girl
Entered the room,
And wonder of wonders —
Came and climbed up on my knee,
Played simple games with me.
She tore a tissue into bits
And gave them to me as gifts,

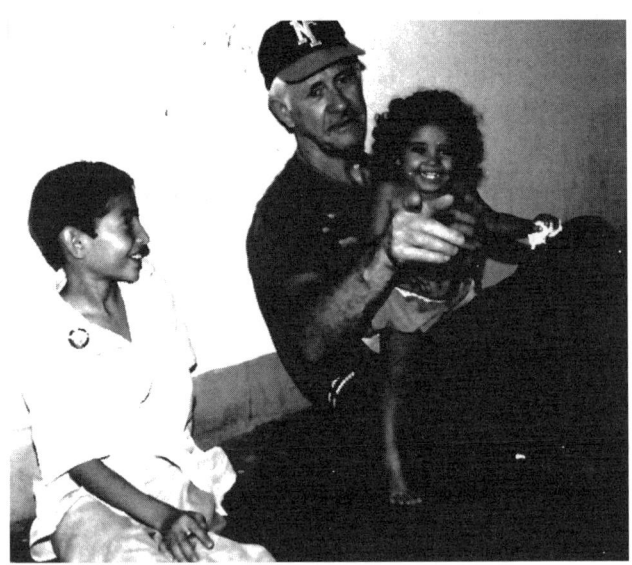

And at that moment
Gold coins would have been
Scorned in their place.

Eventually, by day's end,
The Lord got through to me
And said with kindest words,
"Son, you need to climb into My lap
As that little child climbed into yours.
And you don't need
Letters, titles and such
Behind your name.
I want you to write for Me,
Love as I love,
Touch as I touch.
That's why you're here."

#14

EDGAR GOES HOME

I wrote this while covering a Mercy Ships Orthopedic Team in Honduras in 2000. Join us as we pray for needy children who are often victims of war or other people's decisions and lifestyle.

*** *** ***

"Take him home to die," the doctor said.

The hospital patient in San Pedro Sula, Honduras, doesn't understand the doctor's words, nor does he understand his terminal condition. Edgar Montoya is only seven months old. He has tuberculosis and AIDS, which he contracted from his mother.

Baby Edgar lay in his crib in an isolation room. As I watched through a window, he awoke and began to cry, though I couldn't hear a sound. He caught my eyes and held them, his pleading, mine brimming with tears. When I turned to leave, both of us were weeping. My last view of Edgar was of his tiny, wrinkled arms flailing from his yellow Garfield shirt, his mouth still framing that silent cry.

"Take him home to die," the doctor said.

"Come on Home to live," Jesus said.

#15

AND THEN ... PAULA SMILED

In the summer of 2003, Helen and I traveled to Honduras on a writing assignment. We covered a Mercy Ships' orthopedic team working in the Mario Catarina Rivas Hospital in San Pedro Sula, also known as the "poor man's hospital."

*** *** ***

About nine p.m. in Choloma, Honduras, Antonio and Paula Pacheho and their ten-year-old daughter Maria were ready for bed. A knock came on the door. Antonio hesitated, but someone outside shouted "Police! Police! Open up!"

An honest farmer, Antonio had nothing to hide from the police, so he opened the door. It was a fatal mistake. Seven young men from a street gang burst into the room. Antonio was shot and killed. Paula, shot in the stomach and ankle, collapsed in agony on the floor. Maria climbed out a bedroom window, escaped into the darkness, and found her way to her sister Marianna's house.

Later that night Paula was transported to the emergency room at Mario Catarina Rivas Hospital, where doctors treated her stomach wound. She lay in the emergency room 30 days, and then 21 more days in a crowded hospital corridor. When a Mercy Ships orthopedic team visited Honduras, a surgical team repaired Paula's ankle.

The day before the surgery, Helen & I visited the hospital. Paula said the open sore on her lower back hurt badly whenever she moved. A nurse was called. She looked closely at the inflamed area and discovered a bullet just below the surface! Our orthopedic team leader extracted a .38 caliber bullet. Paula kept it as a souvenir.

*** *** ***

One day soon after that Paula asked Helen to cut her hair, which had received very little attention during her 51

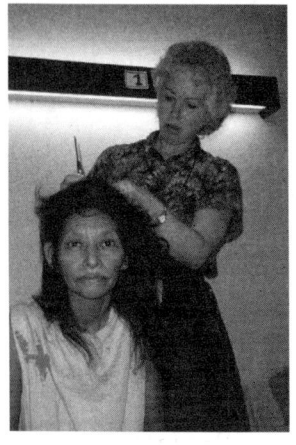

days in bed. That request was somewhat like asking Billy Graham to preach! Helen has been our family barber for over 50 years, and often cuts friends' hair as well. A time for Paula's glamour haircut was arranged.

Barbering a patient with two bullet wounds in a hospital bed posed some new challenges. As Paula reclined in bed, her daughter Marianna and Helen gently washed her hair. Using several basins, they carried water from a small sink on a distant wall. They did a fine job, though the floor rather reminded me of the deck of the Mercy Ship during a storm!

Finally, Paula sat up again and Helen cut out the matted tangles, then she and Jessica carefully combed out Paula's long black hair. While locks of hair fell away, bits and pieces of their story came together. Antonio and Paula have eight children. Paula and youngest daughter Maria will stay with her married daughter Marianna when she leaves the hospital. Paula's dirty and broken toenails speak volumes about hard work on their farm.

After Helen created attractive bangs on Paula's forehead, I teased her that she would look like a teenager again. Okay, so I stretched it a bit! Paula is 54 and when she smiles you can see all her front teeth are either missing or just rotten stubs. We then found out that the 5,000 Lempira ($294 USD) the gang members stole that fateful night was set aside for two things: Antonio had a dream of owning a cow, and Paula hoped to get her teeth fixed.

When Helen was nearly done with the haircut, she said, "Paula, I'm curious, why did you ask me for a haircut, when you hardly know me?" Her answer revealed how far a small act of kindness can go.

Paula asked, "Remember the very first day you visited me? I was in a lot of pain when you stopped by and held my hand. You talked to me kindly, and it made me so happy. I wanted a haircut to have something to remember you by."

The haircut was finished, the floor swept, and it was time for Paula to look in the mirror. Would she like it? Her hair was shorter, layered, bangs in front—maybe she would be disappointed. Since the only mirror was over the small sink on the wall, Paula got out of bed, and refusing any help, she hopped on her one good leg to the mirror. We held our breath, and then ... Paula smiled.

*** *** ***

A few days later, our Mercy Ships' van pulled off the main road into Choloma and we looked for a small green house. After a couple wrong turns, then a left at a building spray-painted with gang graffiti, we found Paula's daughter Marianne's house. The hospital provided a bodyguard when we traveled on medically related visits, and now, armed with a shotgun, he took up his position nearby. We entered a small one-room wooden house that seemed to be home for seven people and an unknown number of termites.

Paula reclined on a cot in the corner. The room was already stifling hot, even though it was only mid-morning. Our translator said, "Paula, we are here for two reasons—first, we want to see how you are.

Paula and her daughters and grand-daughters.

Second, we heard the gang stole all the money you intended for your teeth. The Mercy Ships' team took an offering this morning and we arranged with a dentist in San Pedro Sula to get your dental work done. It won't cost you anything. We can take you into town today if you want to go, and he can get started."

Paula seemed a little bewildered as she took it all in. She sat up and looked at her daughter Marianna for reassurance, and then … Paula smiled.

#16

THE ROCK

If you're reading this, you survived the global Covid pandemic in the early 2020's. A sense of urgency and fear gripped the nation. Differing views and opinions bombarded us daily.

I desperately needed to counteract that atmosphere with deep quietness of spirit. In my heart I wanted to live at peace with myself, to have an inner shelter, a refuge from the storm. I yearned for that relationship, in the quietness of the secret place, the inner chamber.

*** *** ***

In Yemen, where Helen and I once worked as missionaries, I sometimes saw huge boulders along the road, ten or fifteen feet in diameter. In one particularly enormous rock, someone had laboriously chiseled a door, and then tunneled onward into the center, until they had a chamber, a home within the rock itself.

I never stopped my old Ford truck and asked those gathered nearby if I could see or enter their home. I wish I would have. I can imagine the quiet interior, the feeling of solid shelter from the storms and the elements. It must have emanated a feeling of strength and security.

That is what I want in God. A place to come in from the storm, to find shelter and peace. I don't mind the battle, whatever it may be. But sometimes a soldier must just draw back and enter the Rock, to find quiet rest. Does God have a place like that, a place where I can pause for rest?

*** *** ***

It needn't be long, Lord, and I'll be out there again with the rest of Your army. I know You understand. I'll do my best today to soldier on for You. Thank You for the memory of the rock along the road in Yemen.

In a very real sense, I believe I am sheltered by the Rock of Your love and provision. Even when I don't know it, Your hands hold me and shelter me on all sides. They cover me over. Today I enter that rest, that place of quietness, strength, and solitude. Thank You for being my God, my Rock.

#17

CANADIAN RESCUE

Pulled from the frigid waters of a Canadian lake, the patient lay on the ground, desperately gasping for air. I must do CPR or chest compressions immediately, or my rescue efforts so far would all be in vain. But which kind? Or should I do mouth-to-mouth resuscitation?

*** *** ***

At the young ages of 18 and 20, Helen and I arrived in the wilderness of northwest Ontario, Canada, a month after we married. The throb of the engine on the Cessna 180 float plane was music to my ears. The pilot made a perfect landing on the lake's surface, and we turned and taxied to the dock. Fellow missionaries were there to tie down the plane and greet us.

So began an idyllic two years in the Canadian "bush." We joined a staff of 20 committed people at a boarding school for

50 Ojibway and Cree Indian children, grades Kindergarten through 8th. Helen helped teach and I worked in all things physical: fell trees, made floating log booms, cut logs on our sawmill, did construction, plus helped gather 50 cords of firewood a year for the Mission Station during the long, cold winters. Once it reached 56 degrees below zero Fahrenheit.

Many of my fun activities during this time centered around hunting, fishing, and exploring the deep woods surrounding us. One day I had the bright idea of making myself a Daniel Boone hat. Made from the skin of a raccoon, with tail hanging down over the shoulders, it seemed like a grand endeavor. Trouble was, there were no raccoons that far north. We had plenty of skunks though, so I thought that would suffice.

Someone on the base loaned me a live trap, a cage-like rectangular wire box with a door on both ends. When an animal steps on the trigger plate in the center, the doors drop and lock. I set and baited the trap near the mission's vegetable garden. In the morning I had a large skunk. One of my friends told me that if I took a large blanket and walked slowly up to the trap and laid the blanket gently over skunk and trap, he would not spray me.

It worked! I walked triumphantly home, carrying trap, skunk, and blanket about a quarter mile back to our cabin. I was careful not to stumble and drop the trap. My Daniel Boone hat was almost a reality.

Then common sense set in. If I shot the skunk, he would spray. I didn't want a hat that smelled like a skunk forever. Could I drown it? I had never heard of anyone doing that ... but it was worth a try.

I took the trap, blanket, and skunk, down to the lake. I carefully submerged the trap, then pulled off the wet blanket. Through the wire sides of the trap, I watched the skunk frantically pacing from one end of the trap to the other, desperate to get out. Then he started to slow down and moved slower and slower. By then, I was beginning to feel sorry for it, so I lifted the trap out of the water. The skunk lay on the bottom of the cage, barely alive. I opened one door of the trap and dumped the sodden skunk on the ground.

Now let's return to my story's beginning ... "The patient lay on the ground, desperately gasping for air." Still feeling sorry for it, I turned the skunk on his back and began pushing down on his chest with my two thumbs. Water came out of his mouth, as air went in. In a couple minutes I could see he was going to make it. When he was conscious enough to turn over on his own, he slowly got to his feet and stumbled off into the brush, dragging his tail on the ground like a black and white wet mop.

So, I'm probably the only person you know who ever gave CPR to a skunk. Mind you, now, it was *not* mouth-to-mouth resuscitation! If you repeat this story, be sure to get it right. I may be crazy, but I ain't dumb!

#18

MMMM ... MAYONNAISE

The annual conference of the Missionary Baptist Church in Burkina Faso, West Africa, included good speakers, encouraging reports from the field and delicious food. During an afternoon luncheon, the women in attendance raved about the homemade mayonnaise used in the sandwiches. The chef was called in to share his recipe and reveal how he made the tasty mayonnaise.

Midway during his demonstration, the chef took a large mouthful of peanut oil. Both hands were occupied by holding the bowl and mixing spoon, so at three or four opportune moments he squirted peanut oil from his mouth into the mayonnaise batter! Much to the chagrin and dismay of his gathered audience, what tasted so good a few moments before, suddenly lost its appeal.

Life is like that. Physical food that tastes so good loses its appeal when we find out it really isn't good for us. Television, videos, movies and much in the media and digital world deadens our sense of right and wrong.

Ask yourself this question: What is todays' culture and society spitting into your bowl of values and beliefs?

Be careful what you put in your mouth, and in your mind. But enjoy your mayonnaise and the gift of taste God gave you. Psalm 34:8 (KJV) says, "O taste and see that the Lord is good! Blessed is the man that trusts in Him."

#19

SPARKLING CLEAN AND STREAK FREE

My heroic wife narrowly averted a terrible disaster last night. All transpired while I slept, blissfully unaware of the unfolding drama in the winter night.

I went to bed at my usual 8 p.m., since I am up well before dawn. Helen was still reading a book, sitting comfortably on the floor in warm proximity to the fireplace. We prayed together, as is our custom. Alas, I did not know danger lurked so close at hand! About midnight, when I got up to visit the bathroom, she awoke and told me her harrowing tale.

When she tired of reading, she got up from the floor to head for bed. She happened to look at a block of oak firewood sitting nearby that I brought in for the night fire. What she saw sent chills of alarm up and down her spine, even though she stood in front of a blazing fire. Dear reader, I can hardly go on and describe what she saw! Pardon me a moment while I collect my strength and firm my resolve. And please sit down before reading any further.

What she saw on the block of firewood were hundreds, no—maybe thousands of ants! Scientifically speaking, we can assume they were Fire Ants, since they were so close to the fire. They were frenziedly crisscrossing the block of wood, madder than hornets. Some had dropped to the floor, and were closing ranks, ready to march through the house, stinging everyone in their path. I could easily have died in my sleep last night, but for the quick thinking of my lion-hearted wife.

We have a supply of Ant & Roach Killer under the kitchen sink. Helen, in a state of frenzy herself, grabbed what was nearest at hand. She sprayed and sprayed—and sprayed some more. She began sweeping up ants and throwing them in the fire. Then she left me a note on the floor beside the empty spray can with a note that said, "This block of firewood had ants on it!"

At 4 a.m., when I got up, there were no ants anywhere. Perhaps a small remnant of sparkling clean and streak free ants escaped and hid under the baseboard, mortally afraid of the madwoman with the spray can of 409 Glass Cleaner!

#20

UNITED AIRLINES FLIGHT 950

As I crossed the Atlantic on U.A. Flight 950 from Washington DC to Brussels, Belgium, the crew began to serve a meal. The steward tried to get the attention of the lady passenger, ahead of me, to no avail. When he started to move on, she suddenly saw him and said, "Why am I not getting a meal? I want a meal!"

He apologized and said, "I asked you three times if you wanted something to eat and you never responded! You had those ear buds in your ears, and I guess you couldn't hear me."

"Why didn't you touch me?"

"We aren't allowed to touch passengers," he answered.

Gradually, the tension lightened. The steward served her a meal and moved on and the lady ate her lunch.

I have given some thought to that incident ... how does God get our attention when we are distracted? He wants to serve us daily bread and generous portions of His grace, goodness, mercy, and blessings. Do we sometimes have in our earbuds of busyness and don't hear Him say, "Come to Me, you who are weary and heavy laden, and I will give you rest."

He waits beside you in the aisle, even now, and will answer your call. Unlike the airline steward, He will, if necessary, touch us ... with something that gets our attention. Remember that He is a loving God and always has our best in mind.

POSSUM DANCE

#21

Ready to leave the house at 5:10 a.m. for my early morning run, I saw the motion light come on outside. I eased the front door open and looked out. I hoped to see the armadillo that recently dug up my front yard. It was time to administer severe justice—but I'll spare you the details.

Instead of the armadillo, a large possum meandered in my direction. Possums meander, in my opinion, seldom if ever in a hurry, intent on whatever their possum brain focuses on. I stood still in the doorway to see what would happen. He got within three or four feet, then finally saw me, or sensed my presence, and turned to walk away. I decided to help him along and took a couple quiet steps on the sidewalk, ready to give him a boot in the backside.

Just before my right foot connected, he turned and latched onto my foot! Ever have a possum hang on your tennis shoe with his teeth while you did a one-legged dance in the early morning? It probably would have made a Funny Home Video, but funny was not on my mind at that moment. I finally shook him loose, and he wandered off into the bushes, none the worse for wear.

Neither was my shoe the worse for wear, just my damaged sense of propriety—and I'll get over that.

More Important Than a Box

#22

In 2012, Helen and I worked five months at an orphanage in Omoa, Honduras. It was home for 32 girls, ages 4-17. Before we left for Honduras I asked the Lord to break my heart for the orphans. He answered that prayer. Sometime later, when we returned stateside, someone asked us about our family and how many children we had. I replied, "We have two boys ... and 32 girls."

*** *** ***

I made the plywood box with great care, glad for the opportunity to do something for Eva. Out of the 32 girls living at the orphanage in Honduras, 15-year-old Eva was one of the shy ones. An exceptionally gifted artist, she had been befriended by a lady on a work team from the States. She would soon send Eva some art supplies, and she needed something with a padlock to keep her things safe. The box I made for her was one of my last projects at the orphanage before we left for the States and home. When finished, I presented it to Eva, gave her the keys and a hug and said, "God loves you, Eva!"

As I turned to walk away, Blanca, one of several teenage girls who had witnessed the occasion said, "Larry ... "

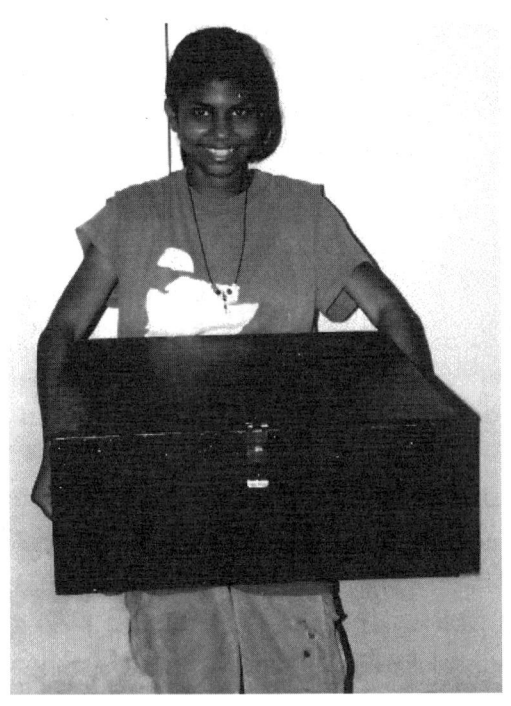

My interruption came quickly because I was sure I knew what she was going to say. "Yes, Blanca, you want a box, too. I'm sure all the girls want a box, but I don't have time to build you one now. We leave the day after tomorrow."

It was then I learned a very important lesson I hope I never forget about judging someone's intentions too quickly.

"No, Larry," Blanca said, "I don't want a box. I just wanted to say that God loves me, too!"

Dumbfounded, I collected my wits and said, "Yes, Blanca, God loves you, too. God loves us all."

And that's more important than a box.

#23
WHEN MERCY COMES FULL CIRCLE

She was caught in the very act of ... skipping school. That may not sound too serious, but in the Honduran orphanage where 15-year-old Mayra lived, it could have dire consequences. Depending on what she did while absent from public school classes, she could be pulled out until age 18! That seemed to us a very harsh punishment, but it was something the directors considered.

Helen and I are in charge of things today as the directors are gone. At midmorning, Mayra sits alone in the backyard under the clothesline, looking dejected and extremely sad. All the other girls are in school. Mayra is grounded until the directors talk with the schoolteachers and evaluate her "crime."

We try to console her. I find some encouraging verses in my Spanish Bible and ask her to read them. She sits on a bench, swinging her feet as she reads them.

It is then I hear the still small voice of the Holy Spirit whisper in my heart, *Wash her feet.*

My heart beats faster. *No way, Lord!*

Wash her feet, the voice repeats.

I told Helen what I thought I heard. I love my wife and her godly wisdom. She said, "If God tells you to do it, then be obedient."

Mayra hides her face in her hands. I take my bottle of drinking water and wash her feet. She cries, and Helen holds her close. *Such hard, calloused brown feet! How many miles, how many soccer games have they played? Where will those feet go when she turns 18 and leaves the orphanage? Only God knows the answer to those questions.*

It was a long day. The other children return in early afternoon. Two of the older girls, Maria and Emerita, get into a fist fight, scratch and bite until I have to separate them. I never imagined girls fought that way! Several other serious problems surfaced before day's end. By evening Helen and I are physically and emotionally exhausted. After supper I tell Helen I plan to go out back of the orphanage for some quiet.

I ease myself down on the grass and review the day. How hopeless it all seems sometimes to instill Christian values in these kids. What will their future hold, anyway? And tonight, why does it all seem so impossible?

Several children leave the building, see me and head my way. One is Mayra, and when she sees me obviously discouraged, she gets her friend Karen and they come and sit down beside me. The concern and kindness on their faces is so evident, I can't help it ... tears begin to slide down my face. *Then Mayra reaches over and carefully wipes the tears away with her hand ... mercy has come full circle.*

Before long, Reynita, Marilyn and Claudia join us. I love to hear the girls sing when I drive them to school in the bus, so I ask if they would sing some songs. For the next 30 minutes they cheer my heart with Sunday School choruses in Spanish plus some fun English songs. I had never before been comforted by "Old MacDonald had a Farm," but it certainly helped tonight!

    Karen catches a firefly and we marvel at its green light. The girls sing a few stanzas of "Edelweiss." My spirit lifts and I join in. Before we get up from that special, anointed place, Karen looks intently at me and asks, "No more crying?" Those words from Karen,

who has known more than her share of tears in life, meant a lot.

"No, Karen," I say with a smile, "no more crying."

I feel a little sorry when Nora, one of the directors, returns at 8 p.m. from grocery shopping in San Pedro Sula. Now Helen and I are free to walk across town to our little rented house. Yes, it has been a long hard day, but it ended well.

And when we eventually come to the end of our journey on earth, I hope to hear the words, "Well done—good and faithful servant, enter into the joy of the Lord." There will be "no more crying" there.

REMEMBERING REYNITA

#24

Reynita looks much like the other girls, ages 4-18, except for a dark discoloration under her eyes. The orphanage directors say it has improved over the years, but the dark rings stubbornly refuse to go away. The doctor claims it's because she was severely malnourished as a young girl. When authorities found Reynita as a small child, she was so hungry she was eating dirt to keep her stomach full. Remembering Reynita helps me resist a second helping of dessert.

When the *Caribbean Mercy* docked in nearby Puerto Cortez, crew members often came to the orphanage to help out on special projects. Before the ship departed we arranged a visit for all the girls. After a tour onboard and an inspirational talk by Captain Jon Fadely, everyone enjoyed cake and ice cream. It was the first time the children ever visited a ship and they talked about it for days.

REDEEMING THE WALL

  The mid-morning sun in Sierra Leone, West Africa, is already uncomfortably hot. A cement mixer rattles and clatters in the background as a half dozen construction workers stand with bowed heads. The men hold an array of worn, sweat-stained straw hats and baseball caps in their hands as the service begins.

  I give a small bottle to Pastor Jalloh. He shakes into his hand a portion of crushed mortar from Germany's infamous Berlin Wall. He then scatters it in the freshly poured cement foundation of the Health Care Clinic as I pray ...

Lord, this crushed and broken mortar represents crushed and broken dreams. It came from a wall that was built to divide German citizens, which separated families and loved ones and brought hurt to many people. Today we symbolically dedicate this portion of the Berlin Wall and the new clinic

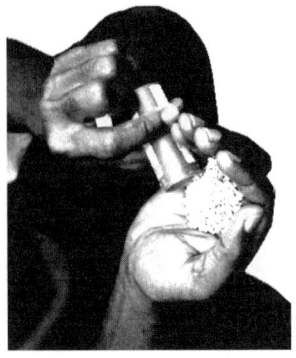
to You. Where there was hurt and pain, use this building to bring healing. Where there was division of people and broken dreams, bring unity, vision, and purpose to the people of Sierra Leone. In His holy name, Amen.

With a murmur of "Amens," the men put on their hats. Dust rises as they shuffle their feet, pick up their shovels and return to work.

*** *** ***

The portion of the Berlin Wall was given to me by a friend who visited soon after it fell. God does indeed take what was meant for evil and uses it for good. He wants to do that in all our lives today.

#26

CHRISTMAS CAROLING

The Caribbean Mercy ship was in Galveston, Texas, on a goodwill tour from December 6, 2001 to January 8, 2002. I was onboard doing ship renovations, so I joined crewmembers one evening for Christmas caroling.

*** *** ***

In the darkness of a cold and windy December evening, a dozen adults and three children gathered on the dock beside the *Caribbean Mercy.* We joined hands in a circle, and several people prayed. I was impressed by the sincere prayer of nine-year-old David. We practiced a couple carols on six crewmembers leaning over the ship rail. They clapped politely.

It was a joy to have the three children along. First grader Miranda was brim full of energy and happiness. David's buddy, 11-year-old Nicholas, jokingly suggested that

David hold out his baseball cap for donations.

We left the dock and walked down Moody Avenue, past a wooden Indian of stern visage, and stopped to sing on a street corner. A man and woman walked by and thanked us for singing. We passed the Galveston Cotton Exchange, established in 1872, and gathered together outside Mikono's Restaurant.

Three ladies who were Christmas shopping came over and joined in the songs and a college-age man with a USC Baseball shirt came out of the restaurant to listen. David immediately went to his side, shared his song sheet and helped him follow along with the words.

A little later, at Bob's Grocery, it was much like a wind tunnel but we sang *Joy to the World* anyway. A tough-looking man came outside, made a phone call, then stood and watched a few minutes. When he left he had a small smile on his face ... or was it a smirk?

At the next street corner a young homeless man in a brown trench coat and wool cap stopped by. His name was Richard and he stood with eyes downcast and listened closely as we sang *O Come Let Us Adore Him.* Two guys from our group put their arms around his shoulders and prayed for him. Tears glistened on his cheeks. As we walked away, Richard repeatedly kissed his fingertips, pointed upward and said, "Peace be with you."

Sewer pipes snaked down the side of an adjoining building and trashcans spilled their contents onto the sidewalk. The neighborhood was definitely getting rougher.

Outside the Cabana Club a woman sat on the wooden front steps. "May we sing a Christmas carol for you?" Deanna asked the lady on the steps.

"It's up to you," she replied in a sad voice, but *Joy to the World* seemed to stir some long-ago memory and she joined in, singing quietly. A very rough looking man came and stood beside her and when we finished he pulled her abruptly to her feet, and they walked away.

Remembering September 11, we wanted to honor the firemen, so we stopped to sing at the local fire station. Eight or nine men in blue listened attentively as we struggled through *O Holy Night.* I thought we should have borrowed one of their extension ladders to reach the high notes!

Farther down the street we approached a house where the yard light was on and a dog barked. No one came to the door while we sang. The dog barked a couple more times, then entered his kennel. He showed no appreciation at all for good singing. A lady at the next apartment warned us to be careful because we were in a drug-pusher neighborhood.

We were tired and on our way back to the ship when we met Edna. She shuffled down 27th Street in old tennis shoes, with multiple layers of coats and a shawl over her head to protect from the cold night air. We could smell alcohol on her breath. We stopped and talked about 20 minutes, then asked if we could pray for her. When we prayed the tears flowed, and she wiped her nose on her sleeve.

We sang *Jesus Loves You* to Edna, as we stood there next to the old La Bahia Bar, which was closed and padlocked with plywood over the windows. Edna certainly needed to know that Jesus loved her. She bobbed up and down as she talked, possibly in pain. She said she had liver cancer.

When we asked if *she* wanted to pray, Edna willingly agreed. "I want to change," she prayed. "I want to be filled with the Holy Ghost." She asked God to forgive her for killing two people and her many other sins. A former heroin addict, she lost custody of her children nine years ago and said she couldn't go home anymore.

How much could we believe of her alcohol-befuddled story? When we finished our prayers, she hugged us all and walked with us toward the ship. After several blocks we paused and Edna talked quietly to us, but mostly to herself, then set off across the street. We stood and watched as she stopped several times, retraced her steps, then turned again and went out of sight.

Poor Edna. Deanna, one of our carolers, wants to take Edna a Bible in the morning.

#27

A Gift for Edna

Edna, whom we met last night while Christmas caroling, said she would be at the Feeding Center for the homeless on Saturday morning. Four of us from the ship set out to find her. Deanna carried her Bible, filled with personal notes, underlined and precious. It had been a gift to her 12 years ago. Today she would give it away to a homeless woman.

Every Saturday morning in the parking lot of the First Presbyterian Church in Galveston, Texas, you can see a sight that will both dishearten and hearten you. There, gathered expectantly, is a group of about 200 homeless people. That's the sad part. This December morning they are bundled in old, tattered clothing in the cold air, and huddled in groups to talk. Then the cars and pickups of the Galveston Street Ministry begin to arrive. The workers wear yellow shirts over their jackets. On the back are the words "Do You Love Me? Feed My Sheep."

And feed them they do—that's the good part. Since 1985 they haven't missed a single Saturday morning. Tables are quickly set up and the aroma of hot food, coffee and donuts wafts over the waiting crowd.

But before the donuts and hot breakfast, ministry workers serve the Bread of Life. Someone in a yellow shirt gets the crowd's attention, and then shares several scriptures and stories. A man sitting on the curb keeps talking loudly.

The speaker stops, makes his way to him, squats down to eye level and asks, "Will you cooperate with me?" He does. After a general invitation to accept Jesus and a prayer of blessing, hot food is dished out to the hungry crowd.

An old rusty Chevy van, filled with junk nearly to the rooftop, pulls up and a man gets out. I introduce myself to him. His name is Roger, and he says he does this every Saturday. Homeless himself except for his vehicle, the man walks to the serving area where he tends the coffee machine. He also helps at Salvation Army and is grounds keeper at a Baptist church. Roger goes on to explain that, "Every Saturday morning I feed the birds the leftovers. Some people don't like it, but the birds need to eat, too!"

A few minutes later a man brought Roger a plate of leftover French toast and eggs. Roger immediately turned and threw the food into the street! A deluge of seagulls, pigeons and grackles descended like a cloud. Roger enjoyed that.

He then gleefully told me "I made the newspaper!" Apparently a news photographer was there recently, took pictures, and Roger was in the paper. I could tell it was a highlight for him.

On the opposite side of the parking lot, another church group offers basic medical care. A woman in the middle of the crowd makes huge soap bubbles over two feet in diameter to entertain the children. Several ladies from the street ministry sing some old spirituals and Christmas carols. A couple of the men, who were probably in church choirs in their better days, join in and sing heartily, even though missing front teeth.

An hour later, as we are about to leave, Edna finally arrives. She looks better this morning, except for a very bloodshot right eye, and seems in good spirits. The alcohol from last night has worn off. She accepts Deanna's Bible, says "Thank you," and tosses it carelessly on a box of clothing, where it nearly slides off onto the pavement.

But does it really matter? Deanna gave Edna her own Bible, first as a gift to God, then to a homeless woman on the streets of Galveston. As we turned and walked away I heard Edna say to a friend, "Those people did something wonderful for me last night with their prayers."

A Good Week for Hunting

#28

It's been a good week for hunting—one wild hog, three armadillos, and ten snakes!

*** *** ***

On Monday evening I came home about dark from cutting down a tree for a friend. I sat down in the lawn chair on our front porch, took one shoe and sock off and shook the sawdust out. I noticed movement under my chair. It was a snake. I stood up to get a closer look and saw not just one snake, but two poisonous Copperheads.

I ran inside to get my .22 pistol with birdshot, and shot both snakes two times, which didn't seem to slow them down much. They went two different directions. Picture me running around with one shoe off and one shoe on, flashlight in one hand and pistol in the other, trying to keep track of two snakes. I located one and shot it the third time. The other snake disappeared.

At this point Helen came home from a ladies' prayer meeting. She expected me in bed asleep, so when I came around the corner of the house with flashlight, pistol, and a mattock, (which I had added to my arsenal,) she was just a *little* surprised! I found the second snake in the flowerbed and killed it with the mattock.

Through the rest of the week I dispatched nine more snakes around the house—eleven altogether. Ten were Copperheads and one Rat Snake. They seem to come out just before dark, probably eating the gecko lizards that frequent our flower beds. I gave up on the pistol and went to a tool for removing asphalt roof shingles. It has a long handle and a straight, sharp blade. One blow cuts a snake in half.

Last night I went to bed, but couldn't sleep, so got up at 10:30 and looked outside with a flashlight. Right on my doorstep was a big Rat Snake. I was so tired of snakes around the house that I killed it, too, something I don't normally do to Rat

Snakes. The next day I plugged several holes in our brick foundation with wire window screen and haven't seen a snake since.

*** *** ***

On Wednesday morning Helen ran out of the bedroom articulating something about an animal across the lake. I jumped up from my chair and looked out the bedroom window. A wild pig slowly walked the shoreline, picking up bits to eat here and there. From the corner of my deck, I shot the pig with my 30-06 rifle. It was a 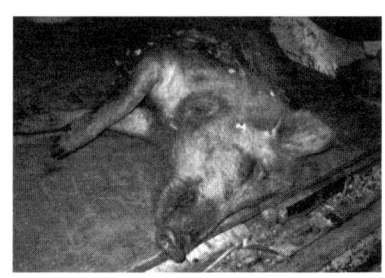 full 100-yard shot and the hog dropped in its tracks at the water's edge.

She was about 200 lbs., a sow ready to give birth. When I butchered her, she had five piglets inside and probably would have farrowed in a couple days. Of course, I've bragged just a little about getting six pigs with one shot! It's the first feral hog I've shot in the wilds, except for a javelina in the hill country around Mountain Home, Texas.

*** *** ***

And the armadillos ... I have an ongoing battle with them. Last summer I killed five, so three so far is about right for mid-July. When it comes to snakes and armadillos, I take no prisoners.

Photo credit: Bradley Mast

ANY POST IN A STORM

#29

I'll admit it ... I had it in for a raccoon this morning. Set me down for a bad attitude, but I had an excuse.

In a conversation with our son Brad last night, he mentioned setting up a small inflatable pool on his deck for their then two-year-old son Joshua to play in. The next morning it was totally deflated. They put up another slightly larger pool, and suspecting foul play, covered it with a tarp. Brad also set up his camera and programmed it to take a picture every minute, all night long.

Sure enough, when Brad and Amy examined photos the next day, they watched a large raccoon trying his best to sink his teeth into the inflated pool. Fortunately, he didn't succeed.

This morning on my early morning run, I came up the sidewalk behind the Mercy Ship's Administration Building. I saw a coon under the streetlight 150 feet away concentrating on catching bugs on the ground that were attracted to the light. His back was to me when I began running in his direction. Moving quietly on the sidewalk, I got within six feet of him before he heard me.

Just before I did my famous game-winning football punt, he took off. The fence around the swimming pool was the nearest thing to climb, so he headed there with me in hot pursuit. He scrambled up the six-foot high fence and turned to snarl and hiss at me. I snarled and hissed back at him and waved my cap in his face. I must have looked ferocious because he decided to abandon his precarious perch on the fence and jumped for the nearby light post. To him it probably looked like a tree.

He managed to scramble up the metal post another eight feet, all the while peeing up a storm! (Or was it peeing down a storm?) Anyway, it looked like a spring rain shower. Then he stopped climbing and looked down at me. I was still waving my cap and pounding on the pole. He slowly lost his grip on the slippery, urine-soaked lamppost. He jumped from 12 feet, hit the ground running, and disappeared in the darkness. Meanwhile, I laughed until my sides ached.

*** *** ***

I have no sympathy for raccoons. I find they're destructive and full of mischief. We once fed them table scraps on our back porch and had as many as nine there at once. (It was more entertaining than TV.) We stopped feeding them some years ago when one came through the screen on the kitchen window at night and helped himself to some fruit on our counter. Today it gave me great satisfaction to scare the pee out of one of them.

#30

FOLLOW DIRECTIONS

I'm the kind of guy who seldom takes time to read directions. I think I can "wing it," and rely on past experience to help me. Sometimes that gets me into trouble.

*** *** ***

Helen and I visited western Canada some years ago when the automatic transmission on my car acted up. It slipped badly, with the possibility of leaving us stranded on the road. I checked the fluid level several times and it read full.

When we stayed overnight with friends in Surrey, British Columbia, I shared my car concerns with our congenial host, Mike Beck, who is an engineer and perfectionist. He read the car instruction manual himself. The manual said, "With engine running, brake engaged, run transmission through all the gears before checking oil level."

Sure enough, when we did it by the book, the dip stick showed two quarts low! After we added the right amount of oil, the transmission performed smoothly again.

Sometimes I bring spiritual or physical trouble on myself because of a lack of proper maintenance. I think I know better, or I'm just too lazy and undisciplined. It's far better to go by The Book, God's Word, and follow all directions and guidelines. Our Master Designer put them there for good reason.

#31

FOLLOW ME

"Surely goodness and mercy
Will follow me ...
All the days of my life." Psalm 23:6

*** *** ***

Father, did You say
Follow me?
Why?
It seems like I
Should be following You,
Your love, goodness, righteousness —
Following hard after You.

*** *** ***

And I do, Lord,
Some days my heart deeply longs
To follow You.
But when cares overwhelm
And stress scratches its fingernails
Across life's blackboard

It's good to remember,
Oh, *so* good to remember
That *You* follow me!
That surely,
As surely as You are God
Your goodness and Mercy
Will follow me
All the days of my life.

Amen

#32

GLUE MAKERS STICKING IT TO US

I discovered a widespread, low-down, highly unscrupulous practice in today's modern world. Someone named Elmer is ripping you off, sticking it to you, and generally taking advantage of millions of little kiddos, or at least their parents, who bought them a glue stick. It's not just Elmer's either, but every manufacturer on the market. Just stick with me for a moment, and I'll explain myself.

Have you ever noticed, when you apply glue with a glue stick, that the last half inch is unusable? You glue away, lost in your own little world of pieces of paper, or photos. You turn the knob one more time, and suddenly—it's all over. No more glue, it's like—finished.

But here's the rub—it's not finished. This is where the glue company makes their profits, multiple thousands of dollars at your expense. The glue stick is designed so that the ordinary consumer throws it away at this point. Someone wants you to leave the last half inch of glue unused because of the evil, diabolical, and fiendish design of the glue stick.

That last half inch of glue is embedded in a little cup-shaped container. Now I've no doubt a glue stick could be designed in such a way that all the glue could be used, but no—the glue company prefers that you just toss it and buy a new one.

Rather than fall for the glue companies' villainous plot, I've devised a way to beat them at their own game. I always keep two glue sticks, and when one runs out, I put it aside and use a new one, until the glue is down an inch or so. Then I turn the new glue stick back down to the bottom and get out my old one. With a pocketknife or something sharp, I dig out all the old glue and put it in the new glue stick. Only then do I throw the old one away. It can be a little messy at times, but it's worth it, in my opinion.

I may be tacky, but I'd rather do that than be taken advantage of by a stickum-up glue company. The whole deception makes me want to paste somebody.

Happy Landing

#33

In 1927, Charles Lindberg flew his plane, *The Spirit of St. Louis*, from New York to Paris. Today it is mounted on the ceiling of the Smithsonian Institute in Washington, D.C.

Back then it was nicknamed the "Flying Fuel Tank," holding 451 gallons of fuel. Because of the large tank, Lindberg couldn't see out the front window, only through the side windows. He flew with a periscope and compass headings.

Lindberg's navigation achievement reminds me of the Christian walk, or flight, here on earth. We don't see so clearly out in front. It's difficult or impossible to look ahead, and we certainly can't see the end of the road. Peering out the side windows at our circumstances doesn't give us a good perspective either.

But these two things I know for certain: I have enough fuel for the journey, and my compass headings are true and sure. When my engine eventually sputters and fails, I'll glide in to a safe and happy landing on the other side. Then I'll meet Jesus, and find out He had His hands on the controls all the time.

#34

I JUST RAN OVER A LITTLE BOY

One of the most rewarding jobs I had while serving on the Mercy Ship Anastasis was leading construction projects ashore. Beginning in Lazaro Cardenas, Mexico, in 1987, we built houses for those who lost their homes in the 1985 earthquake. In later years, from Central America to West Africa, while medical teams did cataract, cleft lip and palate surgeries and much more onboard, our construction teams were busy ashore. We also built latrines, orphanages, an ambulance shelter, and medical clinics, to name just a few things.

*** *** ***

I will share one story from Jamaica. The ship was docked in Port Antonio, on the north coast of the Island. As projects leader, I had two teams at work ashore. I stayed onboard ship during this time, and coordinated details from there, with occasional visits to the field. I had two very capable foremen overseeing the jobs and rested easy with that.

One afternoon I decided to visit the closest jobsite. The 45-minute trip from the *Anastasis* was a bit crazy as everyone drives on the "wrong" side of the road in Jamaica ... a holdover from the earlier English presence on the island. I arrived at the team house about 5:00 p.m. and was met by construction foreman Rich Groff. His first words to me were, "Hey, I'm sure glad to see you! I just ran over a little boy!"

Rich told me the story. He left the job site and drove slowly through the small village. People, dogs and donkeys crowded the narrow road. In his rearview mirror he glimpsed a boy about ten years old, roll out from under the 16-foot trailer he towed. Rich stopped and ran back as a crowd quickly gathered. The crying boy stood up, but appeared in much pain. "Ow! Ow! Ow!" he shouted, tears streaming down his face.

The Jamaicans nearby began to blame Rich. "Whitey! Whitey! It's your fault!"

Then someone from the crowd said, "No, it's not the white man's fault. I saw it happen. The boy tried to jump on the pickup bumper, fell off and went under the trailer."

This news turned the crowd's anger in another direction, and they yelled, "Bad boy! Bad boy!"

Rich walked over to the boy, gently gathered him up in his arms and said, "No, he's not a bad boy. He's just a little boy doing what little boys do!" That calmed the crowd considerably, and they quietly dispersed. The boy hobbled off with his friends and disappeared around a corner.

In the team house, Rich and I talked it over and decided to go back to the village and see what more could be done. We finally located the youngster and later that evening in a doctor's office, x-rays showed no broken bones, only multiple scrapes and bruises.

We found out he was one of nine children who belonged to an unmarried woman who lived in the village. Through this accident a local pastor friend of ours followed up on his recovery. The pastor also shared Jesus with the family and helped with their physical needs.

*** *** ***

Three lessons come to mind from this incident:

- Don't blame people and call names when something bad happens to you. You may not know all the details.

- Show compassion, and lift people up when they're down. Do to others as you want them to do to you.
- Remember, Romans 8:28 says "All things work together for good to those who love Him."

#35

IT'S HERE!

Monrovia, Liberia, West Africa: In late spring of 2007 I was asked to go to the Anastasis in Liberia. The decision had been made to retire the ship and my job onboard was to remove many of the beautiful inlaid carvings and antiquities from the Mediterranean Lounge and other public areas.

*** *** ***

In May the recently renovated *Africa Mercy (AFM)* sailed from Newcastle, England, to join the *Anastasis.* The last ten days before her arrival in Liberia, a poster appeared on the *Anastasis* Reception Whiteboard, telling how many days before the *AFM* was due. Every morning there was a new sticky note on the poster. Excitement built daily as the countdown continued: 7-6-5-4-3-2-1. Finally, in the early dawn of May 23, 2007, the poster in reception read—It's HERE!!

Off the aft deck of the *Anastasis,* in the haze of early morning light, we could see her. Having arrived in the middle of the night, the *AFM* rested at anchor several miles away. Since the poster had  served its purpose, I asked the receptionist if I could have it, and she gladly gave it to me.

Later that day the two ships berthed alongside each other and the transfer of crew and supplies began. It included a ceremonial passing of a torch that a colleague, Walter Schlichting, and I made of materials from the other three ships— *Anastasis, Good Samaritan,* and *Caribbean Mercy.*

In the reception area of the *Anastasis,* I lit the torch and gave it to Chief Medical Officer Dr. Gary Parker. With tears in my eyes, I watched him hand it to someone at the top of the gangway, where it was passed hand to hand down to the dock. Then it went among crewmembers from both ships, in a long circuitous route along the wharf. Four hundred pairs of hands later, our founder Don Stephens received it at the top of the *AFM* gangway.

Photo credit: Esther Biney

I'd also removed and repainted the cross from the bow of the *Anastasis* and it was mounted on the bow of the *AFM*. A new era had begun with abundant and fresh opportunities to show mercy.

The mercy of the Lord is new every morning ... It's HERE!!

#36

KNICKERBOCKER REPORT

In 1962, I played basketball at Western Mennonite High School near Salem, Oregon. Although I was never as good as Al Yoder or Duane Emmert and a lot of other players, for some reason Coach Wally kept me around. Maybe he felt sorry for me.

The boys' basketball team wore white t-shirts and knickerbockers during games. Someone had decided that knickers were modest enough for our conservative school, and it was okay for the fans to see our ankles and lower calves. Unfortunately, the knickers were also a bit tight, at least mine were.

During one always-to-be-remembered game, I went up for a rebound. When I came down with the ball I heard the distinct sound of ripping cloth. I passed the ball off and did a manual inspection of the situation. Sure enough, the entire back seam of my uniform was ripped out! (Using a nautical term—from bow to stern.)

Fortunately, it happened at the end of the court nearest the boys' locker room. I began running backward and hit the swinging door stern first. The door opened with a bang and I went AWOL from the team.

I don't remember if I ever returned for the remainder of the game, but probably not—I was too embarrassed. Most people in the audience didn't even know what happened at the time—until this confessional. Ah, well, they say confession is good for the soul.

LIFE LESSON FROM A SKUNK

#37

One summer day a couple years ago, I got a call from the maintenance manager. A skunk was walking down the road at mid-morning here on the Mercy Ships' property in East Texas. Because I have clearance to use a gun to control the varmint population (armadillos, skunks, and wild hogs), I was asked to dispose of it.

When I met up with the caller, the skunk had just disappeared into a culvert under the road. I could see it some distance away and two shots from my .22 rifle took care of it.

A couple days later I wondered if the skunk may have been rabid since it was out in the daytime and perhaps we should tell the proper authorities. So I found a long pole in my lumber collection, put a hook in the end and went "skunk prospecting."

I was able to drag it out of the culvert and into the nearby field. After two days of

Texas summer heat, the skunk was bloated up like a basketball. Not only did it smell like a skunk, it smelled like a very *rotten* skunk. The Animal Control man wasn't interested in checking for rabies on a rotten skunk, so I left it in the field. An hour later, six vultures were having their dinner. They smacked their lips and looked very pleased with themselves.

*** *** ***

I don't think we fully comprehend the meaning of the word *dead*. In this present day people don't seem to die, they just *pass*. (That word once meant going around a slow moving vehicle on the highway.) In the story of the death of Lazarus, when Jesus arrived in Bethany, Lazarus had been in the tomb four days. When asked to remove the stone, Martha objected and told the Lord, "By this time there is a bad odor." Lazarus was *stinky dead*.

When the apostle Paul said we were *dead* in our transgressions and sins I believe we were *stinky dead*—like Lazarus. Nothing good about us—we were rotten sinners. From this condition God saved us, because of His grace and great love for us.

Even now, though seated in heavenly places in Christ Jesus, sin is always a possibility. We can still be tempted, and we can fall. Some days I detect a distinct odor in my own life and may even swell up with pride or selfish ambition. When I indulge in *stinkin' thinkin'*, and listen to the enemy's lies, I must come quickly to Jesus for forgiveness and cleansing. It's a daily walk for me as I search my heart for sin.

"Search me O God and know my heart, try me and know my anxious thoughts. See if there be any wicked way in me and lead me in the way everlasting," Psalm 139: 23, 24.

That's a life lesson from a skunk.

#38

MEANGUERA ISLAND, EL SALVADOR

Just before daylight on Meanguera Island, there is a subtle mystique of shimmering ocean water and the sound of lapping surf. Fishing canoes surge rhythmically on their tow lines. The darkened coastline slowly reveals houses, clotheslines, and sacks of corn. Two Frigate birds are silhouetted against the gray sky. Roosters somewhere up in the village are conducting a crowing seminar.

The white surf pounds the rocks of Little Meanguera Island across the bay. More Frigate birds go "frigating" by overhead, their narrow tails opening into V's while they maneuver. The eastern horizon presents a beautiful five-minute show of pink before a gray curtain is pulled. Someone must have asked for an encore, because now the pink is back.

With a roar of Evinrudes and Yamahas, fishermen go to work. Three little black-haired, dark-eyed girls in school uniforms of blue, yellow, white, and green, chatter as they come down to the shore. That reminds me we are here for the people, though I won't turn down beautiful scenery.

The smell of wood smoke stings my nostrils and I see the eastern horizon start to blush again just over the small island. In the distant haze, a ridge of Nicaraguan mountains shows dimly, while Honduran hills are closer. If the sun is rising, and I assume it is because the roosters in the village seem to think it necessary, it is hidden behind gray skies, with occasional brush strokes of bright yellows and oranges.

A sunspot grows over Little Meanguera and now it's too bright to look at. People are up, bees buzz, and the day begins. A Mercy Ship's team nurse arrives sleepy eyed for a walk on the beach. Her t-shirt says, "Serving God is not a job, it's an adventure." That's a good thing to remember in mid-afternoon when it's 100 degrees in the shade and you're hot, sticky, and tired.

*** *** ***

DEEP PONDERINGS ON MEANGUERA

> It's the last day of clinic on Meanguera,
> It was a fine sunrise,
> There is a refreshing sea breeze,
> I smell breakfast,
> My socks are finally dry,
> And all is well in the universe!

#39

"Mr. Trace?"

While I sat in the optometrist's waiting room recently, an assistant appeared from a side door, clipboard in hand.

"Mr. Trace?" she called. Getting no response, she raised her voice to carry to the various side alcoves of the large waiting room. "Mr. Trace? Mr. Trace?"

I was about to tell her *There seems to be no trace of Mr. Trace,* when a man suddenly popped up from a distant chair and followed the nurse through the door and down the hallway.

*** *** ***

The search for Mr. Trace reminded me of my own sinful heart. Just when I think I'm doing well and have conquered that besetting, unsettling sin, the Holy Spirit shows up, and calls out, "Just a trace? Just a trace?" Sure enough, up pops a little fear, anxiety, and worry. Or just a trace of bitterness, anger, or critical spirit. When confronted, they duly identify themselves and I usher them down the hallway to the altar of confession and cleansing.

Dear Lord, please erase every trace of sin in my life, that I may serve you more fully and effectively all of my days. Amen.

"If we confess our sins, He is faithful and just and will forgive us our sins and purify us from all unrighteousness" I John 1:9.

Pepsi Generation

#40

The *Island Mercy* drops anchor in the small bay of a remote island in the South Pacific. A necklace of white sand beach wraps itself around the emerald green jungle. Palm trees overlook the rolling surf and birds call to each other. Surely the people of this island will not have been touched by the advances of the modern world!

Yet, as the medical team scrambles from the ship's lifeboat onto the hot sands of this isolated tropical paradise, a remarkable sight emerges ... a Pepsi can lies half buried in the sand. Was it thrown from the deck of a passing cruise liner? Possibly. But more than likely it came from the island, where we soon found soft drinks readily available.

Soft drink companies have succeeded in reaching the most remote corners of the earth. Why have they succeeded where the church has failed? There will probably be no medical supplies in the small clinic on the island. The little school meeting under a thatched roof will have no textbooks relevant to the subjects taught and there will be no church in the village, but the local canteen will be well-stocked with a variety of soft drinks. The children will know the name Pepsi but they will not know the name Jesus.

We want to change that. Each team that leaves the *Island Mercy* is trained in primary health care and evangelism. Although crew will help anyone needing aid, they feel a special concern for women and children. An increasing number of children are sexually abused and many are malnourished.

In a desire to be "modern," some mothers in developing countries stop nursing their babies too soon and instead use popular baby bottles. Yet, in primitive conditions, these bottles are nearly impossible to keep sterile. Milk sours quickly in temperate conditions and infants refuse to drink, or if they do, they often become sick.

Sometimes soft drinks, sugar water, cold coffee or sweet tea are substituted for milk.

On this day the dental team sets up a portable unit ashore while more complicated problems are treated on board the ship. Early every morning, men, women and children walk for miles or come by boat to see the dentist. Health care teams do all they can to alleviate pain and suffering, some of it caused by products of western capitalism.

The late afternoon sun sinks toward the sea and a cool breeze brings refreshment to the tired but fulfilled medical team. They look forward to a night's rest in preparation for another day of ministry. One of the precious little girls stops by, clutching a Pepsi in her hand.

Who will reach the Pepsi Generation? Who will go? Doctors, dentists, nurses, mechanics, carpenters, housekeepers, deck hands, engineers, teachers, and many others will go. They will help the people and share the good news of Jesus.

Would you like to join us? The *Island Mercy* has been retired, but we have other ships, and I'm sure we can find a job just for you. We are ordinary people—we even drink Pepsi sometimes. We have our good days and our bad days. But we have an extraordinary message that really needs to reach the remotest areas of the world. Pepsi has done it … will we?

#41
PECANS & PERSEVERANCE

Last fall, Helen and I gathered some pecans from a friend's back yard. In the evenings, I shelled them in my shop, with visions of pecan pies dancing in my head.

One morning it seemed like some of the unshelled pecans were gone. After the second night I was sure of it, so I set a rat trap and the next day I had the culprit ... a fat pack rat! I looked around for the missing nuts, but there were lots of places he could have hidden them. I knew I'd find them eventually if they were in my shop.

Sure enough, the next time I emptied the old Hoover that I use as a shop vacuum, there were the nuts. Ninety nuts, to be exact ... all mixed in with sheetrock dust and wood chips. I was impressed with the rat's perseverance! He had to climb up some cardboard boxes to get into the container of nuts on my table saw, then return to the floor, go over to the shop bench and up on some cement bags to the shelf where the vacuum was—45 trips a night for two nights. He was serious, persistent, and committed to his task.

No, we didn't throw the nuts away ... Helen rinsed them well in bleach water and dried them in the oven, and I resumed cracking them. They may still turn into a pecan pie someday soon. Come on over for pie and ice cream!

#42

TELLTALE TAIL TRAIL

The forty head of Holstein milk cows that walked from the farthest fields to the big yellow barn on the hill cut deep paths in the pastureland. As a young boy, I often followed cow tracks on muddy trails. Across the fields, through the woods, there was always a trail for my feet to follow.

When I was about ten Pop gave me a .22 rifle. I roamed the farmlands and woods with our two dogs, Shep and Lassie, and hunted squirrels, skunks, porcupines and birds. I wanted to become a "government tracker," like in the comic books I read, and follow outlaws across the prairies. I planned to get rich when I caught an outlaw and turned him over to Wild Bill Hickok, or the Texas Rangers.

As an adult I've tracked my share of big game. Deer, elk, moose and caribou in Alaska, all leave distinctive tracks. In the mountains of Montana, I've looked down on dinner-plate-sized bear tracks in the snow, and hoped the bear wasn't anywhere nearby.

When my wife and I moved to the Mercy Ships Office in East Texas, I became acquainted with wild hog tracks. Also called feral hogs, they are notorious for large scale destructive digging in pastures and woodlands, and can be dangerous.

The armadillo, on a smaller scale, has thoroughly aggravated area homeowners, digging up plants, flowers and lawns. Sometimes an ambitious armadillo's work can even be mistaken for a wild hog. Except for one thing: the armadillo leaves a distinct mark in the freshly turned earth, a furrow from his hard, scaly tail as it drags behind him. I call it his telltale tail trail.

*** *** ***

As I look back on my life, I can see some tracks that mark my spiritual journey. Sadly, one sharp imprint in my spiritual trail is my capability for taking offense. Someone says something, and I take it wrongly. I am hurt by another's words, actions, perceived attitude, or tone of voice. Like the armadillo, I've left a tail trail across years of relationships, sometimes scarring potentially pleasant places, or ruining growing gardens of good will. Most are forgiven and healed, and a few I'm working on now.

The Bible says "Love is not easily offended and keeps no record of wrongs." My goal is to live a life so completely filled with His love and mercy that I never again leave a telltale tail trail of taking offense.

THE BLAME GAME

A friend of mine drove to work one morning on a curvy, winding Texas road. Another vehicle caught up to her and pulled close behind. Mary Beth drove the speed limit and the pickup couldn't pass because of oncoming traffic or double yellow lines. For ten miles the vehicle tailgated her.

They finally arrived at a major intersection with a stoplight. The pickup pulled up beside Mary Beth and the driver motioned for her to roll down her window. With sarcasm and anger the man said, "Thank you for making me late to work this morning!"

*** *** ***

Sometimes we must endure rudeness, but we don't need to buy into blame that isn't ours. Jesus was accused of many things. When appropriate He responded with truth. At other times, He held His peace. We must live close enough to the Father that we will know precisely the right response in every situation.

Proverbs 19:11 says, "A person's wisdom yields patience; it is to one's glory to overlook an offense."

The Doctor Is In

People often greet me in passing with the question, "How are you?" I don't quite know how to respond to this greeting. Do they really want to know the state of my health or is it just their way of saying "Hi"?

I usually find it's the latter and if I answer, "Good morning," no further inquiries follow as to how I really am. On the other hand, I once heard a friend say, "I asked her how she was, and I got a 45-minute organ recital!" I guess you've got to be careful.

I am trying to think of a creative response to the "How are you?" greeter. Something like "I'm under a doctor's care—have you heard?" That should get their attention. Then, when I think they look sufficiently concerned, I'll tell them, "Yes, the doctor's name is Jesus. He's also called the Great Physician. I have an appointment with Him everyday, in fact multiple times a day. I never sit long in the waiting room—He takes me right in. He even makes house calls, at all hours of the day or night. His bedside manner is great—He sat beside my bed through many a sleepless night.

"Some days He's quite intent on surgery, cutting away sin that has started to grow like a cancer on my spirit. I am grateful for these times, even though it may be painful. I know His diagnosis is always correct, and I never need to get a second opinion.

"Are you sad? He'll pour in the oil of gladness. Discontented? He has a special ointment called contentment. You rub it on the rash of frustration, irritation, and other troublesome symptoms. It works well with regular application."

*** *** ***

Actually, I do have a terminal condition called "life," and the only known cure is "death." Adam's sin caused it. I guess you could call the disease "Adamsinosis."

It's fatal but not final. If you know Jesus, the Great Physician, you'll be ushered right through the waiting room and into His presence, to a place of glory and splendor unimaginable to our finite mind. It's a place where there is no more sickness or pain, sorrow or sadness or death, and we'll live forever in the presence of the King.

Incidentally, I doubt if He will ask "How are you?" because He made you and knows you inside and out. Besides that, He loves you.

#45
THE MAN IN THE RED CAR

A red car pulled up beside me in the Wal-mart parking lot and a man rolled down his window. He had a convoluted, hard luck story, three dollars left and needed to get to his sister's place 75 miles away. His gas tank was empty. Would I give him some money?

I asked him a couple questions and wondered if any money I gave him would go for gas. Or would it be alcohol or drugs? I sent up a silent prayer for wisdom and seemed to sense the Lord's guidance.

"Follow me to the gas pump," I said.

The cashier took my money and the man in the red car pumped his gas. He said he wanted to pay me back. "What's your address?"

"Forget it," I said. "Do something for somebody else sometime." I would rather it be a gift than make him owe me.

He murmured "Thank you," shook my hand and drove away.

This true story is as common and ordinary as Wal-mart. You don't have to be on the "mission field" in order to hear God or be used by Him. Although I didn't "witness" to the man in the red car, I pray God will draw him to Himself. And may my small act of kindness be a part of that process.

The Story of the Anchor

#46

Some people have wondered about the large anchor along Texas Highway 110 at the main entrance to Mercy Ships. Where did it come from? What is its history?

In 1989, the Mercy Ship *Good Samaritan* anchored for the night in St. Marc's Bay, just off the coast of Haiti. In the morning the ship prepared to hoist anchor and sail to La Gonave Island. Captain Al Bennett was on the Bridge and Tim Tretheway on the Fo'csle* as they prepared to sail, but for some reason the *Good Sam's* anchor wouldn't come up. Tim set the anchor brake and Captain Al called for "Engine ahead, dead slow."

They broke loose, and when the ship's anchor surfaced, Tim shouted, "Hey, we're tied on to something!" The *Good Sam's* anchor chain had wrapped several times around the shank of an old rusty anchor.

The *Good Samaritan* moved out of the shallow bay and two scuba divers went overboard. A cable from the ship's crane was attached to the old anchor to take the strain. The *Good Samaritan's* anchor chain then untangled, the old anchor was hoisted

onboard and lowered into the hold. The sail to La Gonave continued without incident.

When the ship returned to the USA, photos of the anchor plus details and drawings were sent to a Maritime Museum in Maine. They said it was an anchor from a French frigate, over 250 years old. One possible scenario is that during the sudden Haitian slave revolt of the late 1700's, the captain cut the anchor free and made a quick departure from St. Marc's Bay. The anchor has detailed drawings on it, plus its

weight (2007 lbs.), and the name of the man who forged it.

When the *Good Sam* arrived in Orange, Texas, I went to the ship with a flatbed trailer and transported the anchor to the International Office in Garden Valley. It attracted quite a bit of attention whenever I stopped, especially as I got farther inland. When people asked me what I was going to do with it, I answered, "I'm going fishing, and I need an anchor. When I find a good fishing hole, I'll drop it over the side of my boat." For some reason, no one believed me!

*** *** ***

In Hebrews 6:18-20, Paul encourages us to ... *take hold of the hope offered to us, (salvation in Jesus Christ) that we may be greatly encouraged. We have this hope as an anchor for the soul, firm and secure. It enters the inner sanctuary behind the curtain, where Jesus, who went before us, entered on our behalf.*

I am thankful that Mercy Ships shares this hope of the Gospel worldwide. I am also thankful we can know this hope of the Gospel personally, so that even in troubling times it remains an anchor for our souls. Our "anchor chain," is wrapped securely around the anchor of God's love.

Fo'csle is short for Forecastle

#47

WHEN WORDS FAIL YOU

Communication is an imperfect art, at best. But when you get *really* tired, well, anything can happen. Consider this incident on the *Africa Mercy*.

My wife and I were nearing the end of a six-week work project on the Mercy Ship. Before we left, there was a group picture planned for the six people serving onboard from our local church in Tyler, Texas. This included eye surgeon Dr. Glenn Strauss and his wife Kim, Helen and I, Allison Greene, and David Cherry. (right to left)

This particular evening, after a hard day's work, Helen and I were in our cabin. Helen was on the phone with David, finalizing details for next day's photo op. I was sitting on the couch, only half listening. It was only later that I heard David's part of the conversation. He had asked Helen if he should "dress up" for the picture.

Now David is a casual but always sharp dresser and Helen meant to respond, "David, I've never seen you underdressed." But what came out was: "David, I've never seen you undressed."

I suddenly perked up. "Helen, what did you say? You've never seen David undressed?"

When Helen realized her faux pàs, she was of course, aghast, and started to apologize. I think she wanted to say, "I'm sorry, I got my tongue twisted." Or maybe: "Oh no, I really stuck my foot in my mouth!" What she said next was, "Oh, David, I'm sorry, I didn't mean that! Oh no, I really stuck my tongue in my mouth!"

From the couch, I offered her this helpful observation: "Isn't your tongue already in your mouth?"

Like I said, communication is an imperfect art. So today, as you walk down life's pathway, be sure to put your best tongue forward.

To contact the author, go to:
www.LarryMast.com